Whiskers and Wishes
A Valentine's Day Story

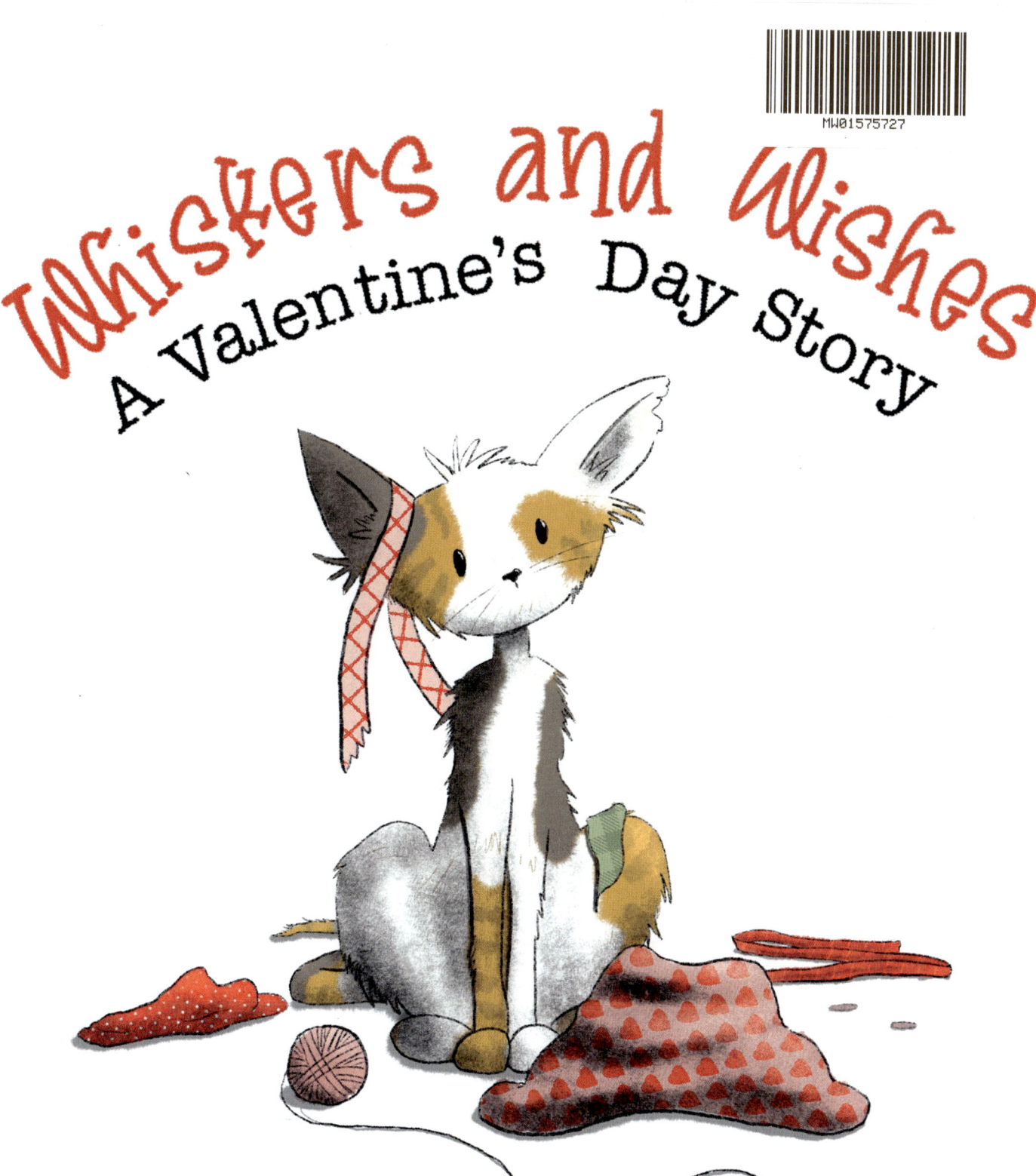

www.mukipress.com
© 2026 by Christine Dillard. All rights reserved.

In the gloom of an alley, a cat sat alone,
Without a name or a place of her own.

She wandered the streets looking for this or for that,
But life offered too little for the lonely cat.

From her perch on a ledge, she viewed the scene,
As families gathered—all happy and keen.

On Valentine's Day, there was laughter and cheer.
Her own world however felt lonely and drear.

"Oh, where is a friend?" she kicked at some rocks,

As she curled up alone in her small box.

But then came a light from apartment three.
The cat spied a girl happy as can be.

Nora was the girl who looked so friendly and fun.
Her laughter made the cat feel as warm as the sun.

Nestled in the coziness of that welcoming space,
Sat a plush kitty-cat with a sweet, smiling face.

With big eyes, it lay on a pillow so soft.
Green with envy, the cat glared down from her loft.

"I could just give that spoiled toy a shove.
Oh, what has it done to deserve so much love?"

With a flick of her paw and a twinge of disdain,
The cat hatched a plan, born from her pain.

She crept in the shadows, and snuck through a crack.
With a glare at the toy, she prepared to attack.

The soft toy made of fluff did not put up a fight.
That didn't stop the cat from showing her might.

The cat clawed at the toy strewn on the floor,
The little girl gasped, "What are you doing? No more!"

The alley cat paused, and time seemed to freeze,
As soft sobs from the girl floated on the breeze.

She dashed to the window, her heart filled with guilt,
Realizing the joy she had shattered and spilt.

Outside on the street, her eye caught a sign,
"Give the gift of love on this Valentine."

The cat sat and pondered, her heart all aglow,
"To make this alright, I must let love grow."

So she gathered some yarn and some buttons galore,
With eager little paws, she raced 'round the floor.

She stitched and she stuffed, giving her all for the toy,
Creating a gift filled with kindness and joy.

A new kitty toy, with a heart stitched in place,
The cat padded up softly, a smile on her face.

Her heart was there, but her belly was a jitter.
For love demands courage of any size critter.

"Oh, my dear cat! You've made me a toy!"
Nora laughed, her heart brimming with joy.

The girl saw the cat turn, head hanging low,
"You tried to make things right—please don't go."

Nora looked at the toy and then at the cat,
"This was made with love, I can see that."

"Valentine is your name from here on out,

So come with me, Valentine," she said with a shout.

So on Valentine's Day, they cuddled and played.
Valentine the cat has a friend to this day.

Made in the USA
Coppell, TX
29 January 2026

70336197R00021